Kids Say and Do the Darndest Things...

Note for Parents:

This journal has been created with different coloured covers: turquoise, yellow, blue, pink, purple and orange, giving larger families the option to have a different coloured journal for each child.

Kids Say and Do the Darndest Things...

By Sharon Purtill

Copyright Dunhill Clare Publishing 2020 All Rights Reserved.

No part of this book may be copied, used, or reproduced in any manner whatsoever without written permission from the publisher, except in a brief quotation embodied in a review or mention.

A Book For Parents to Track All the Wonderful and Crazy Things Their Kids Say and Do

Turquoise Cover Paperback   ISBN: 978-1-989733-48-6
Yellow Cover Paperback   ISBN: 978-1-989733-49-3
Blue Cover Paperback   ISBN: 978-1-989733-50-9
Pink Cover Paperback   ISBN: 978-1-989733-51-6
Purple Cover Paperback   ISBN: 978-1-989733-52-3
Orange Cover Paperback   ISBN: 978-1-989733-53-0

Library and Archives Canada Cataloguing in Publication

Author's Note

One of the greatest things about children is how they see the world. Their wonderment, their curiosity, and the delightful way they express themselves as they interpret everything around them.

The time we have with our children when they are young is short. It wasn't until my own kids were grown and out on their own that I realized how I'd forgotten many of the silly things they said and did. Today, I have only a handful of vivid memories. If I'd recorded those precious moments, documented all the funny things my children did and said in a journal like this, I'd be sitting on a gold mine of wonderful memories.

The years between baby and teen pass so quickly and in those formative years *Kids Say and Do the Darndest Things*. This unique parenting journal was created to help you capture those moments. With it, you can record a treasure trove of lasting memories that you can relive again and again. What a perfect gift to share with your kids once they are adults.

Towards the back of this book, there are some great conversation starters/questions for you to ask your child, perhaps at different ages. I hope that their answers delight you and that you enjoy witnessing their individuality and personality. My wish for you is that this journal becomes the memory keeper of your most treasured moments with your child.

Happy Parenting,

Sharon Purtill

What I love most about you is…

This Book is to Celebrate

_____

Beginning at age:

_____

In celebration of you, I have recorded many of the most
wonderful and crazy things you've said and done.
You've made me smile.
You've made me cry, and you've made me laugh out loud.
And through it all, I have loved you!

Kids Say and Do the Darndest Things…

Age:

Date:

Age:

Date:

Age:

Date:

Age:

Date:

Age:

Date:

Kids Say and Do the Darndest Things...

Age:

Date:

Age:

Date:

Age: Date:

Age:

Date:

Age:

Date:

Kids Say and Do the Darndest Things…

Age: Date:

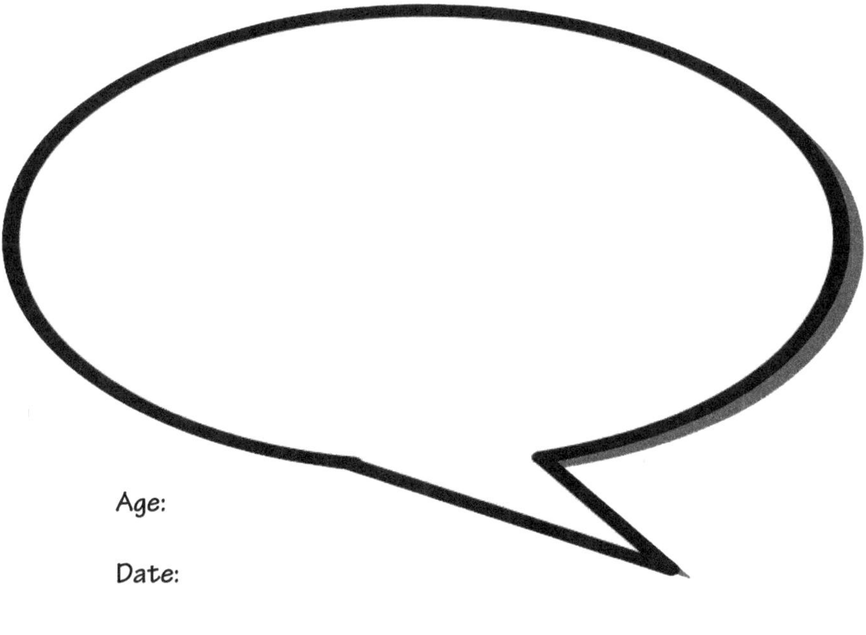

Age:
Date:

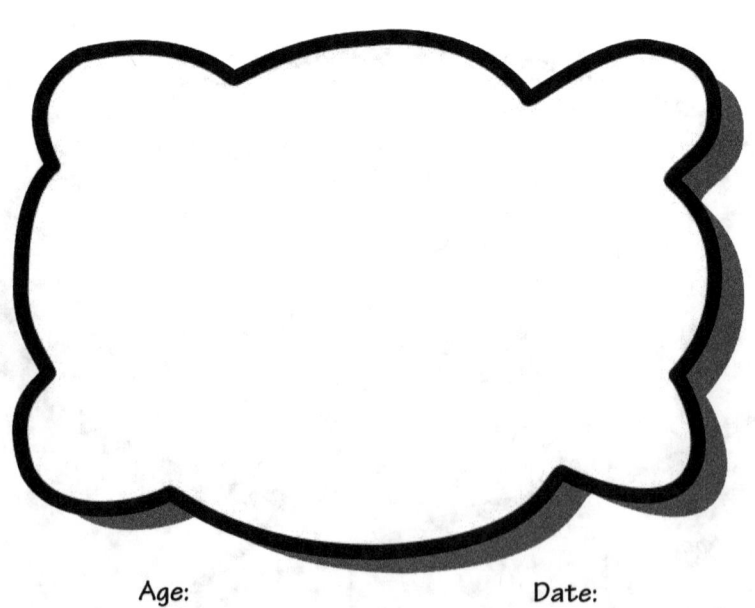

Age: Date:

Kids Say and Do the Darndest Things…

Age:

Date:

Age:

Date:

Age:

Date:

Age:

Date:

Age:

Date:

Kids Say and Do the Darndest Things...

Age:

Date:

Age:

Date:

Age:

Date:

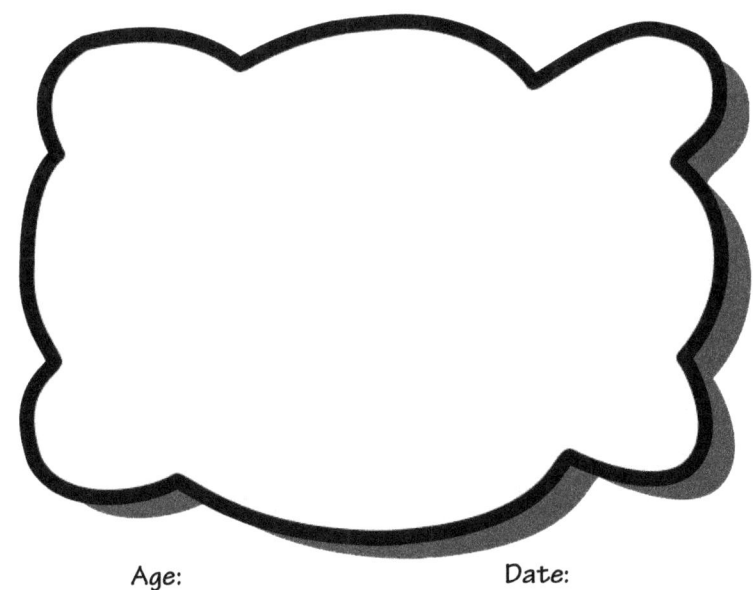

Age: Date:

Age:

Date:

Kids Say and Do the Darndest Things...

Age: Date:

Age:

Date:

Age: Date:

Age:

Date:

Kids Say and Do the Darndest Things…

Age:

Date:

Age: Date:

Kids Say and Do the Darndest Things…

Age:

Date:

Age:

Date:

Age: Date:

Age:

Date:

___
___
___
___
___
___
___
___
___
___
___

Age:

Date:

Kids Say and Do the Darndest Things...

Age:

Date:

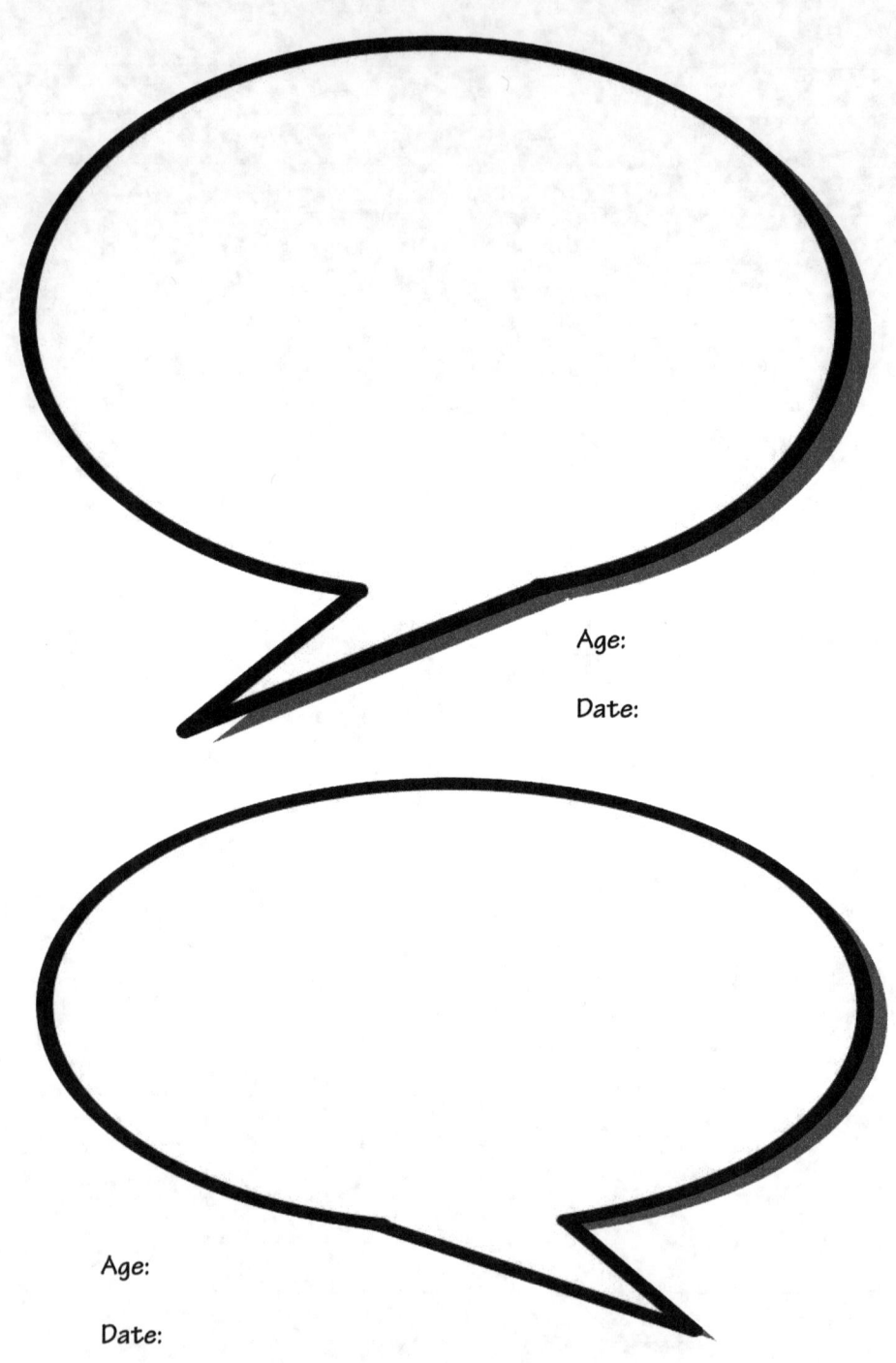

Age: Date:

Age:

Date:

Age:

Date:

Kids Say and Do the Darndest Things...

Age:

Date:

Age:

Date:

Age:

Date:

Kids Say and Do the Darndest Things...

Age:

Date:

Age:

Date:

Age: Date:

Age:

Date:

Age:

Date:

Conversation Starters

Who is your favorite person and why?

Age: Date:

_____
_____
_____
_____

Age: Date:

_____
_____
_____
_____

Age: Date:

_____
_____
_____
_____

Age: Date:

_____
_____
_____
_____

What do you enjoy doing more than anything else and why?

Age: Date:

Age: Date:

Age: Date:

Age: Date:

What makes you happy?

Age: Date:

_____
_____
_____
_____
_____

Age: Date:

_____
_____
_____
_____
_____

Age: Date:

_____
_____
_____
_____
_____

Age: Date:

_____
_____
_____
_____
_____

What makes you sad?

Age: Date:

___

Age: Date:

___

Age: Date:

___

Age: Date:

Tell me about the coolest thing you've ever done?

Age: Date:

_____
_____
_____
_____

Age: Date:

_____
_____
_____
_____

Age: Date:

_____
_____
_____
_____

Age: Date:

_____
_____
_____
_____

What do you want to do when you grow up, and why?

Age: Date:

Age: Date:

Age: Date:

Age: Date:

What kind of house will you live in when you grow up? What does it look like?

Age: Date:

Age: Date:

Age: Date:

Age: Date:

What does your perfect day look like?

Age: Date:

Age: Date:

Age: Date:

Age: Date:

What do you love most about yourself?

Age: Date:

___

Age: Date:

___

Age: Date:

___

Age: Date:

If you wanted to make new friends what would you do?

Age: Date:

Age: Date:

Age: Date:

Age: Date:

What do you think of homework? Why do you think teachers give it out?

Age: Date:

___

Age: Date:

___

Age: Date:

___

Age: Date:

If you were a teacher for a day, what would you teach your students?

Age: Date:

Age: Date:

Age: Date:

Age: Date:

How are you and I alike? How are we different from each other?

Age: Date:

_____
_____
_____
_____

Age: Date:

_____
_____
_____
_____

Age: Date:

_____
_____
_____
_____

Age: Date:

_____
_____
_____
_____

If you could have any superpower, what would it be and why?

Age: Date:

Age: Date:

Age: Date:

Age: Date:

What would you do if you had a million dollars?

Age: Date:

_____
_____
_____
_____

Age: Date:

_____
_____
_____
_____

Age: Date:

_____
_____
_____
_____

Age: Date:

_____
_____
_____
_____

What do you dream about at night?

Age: Date:

Age: Date:

Age: Date:

Age: Date:

If you could be any animal, what animal would you want to be and why?

Age: Date:

Age: Date:

Age: Date:

Age: Date:

What is the next thing you would like to learn?

Age: Date:

___

Age: Date:

___

Age: Date:

___

Age: Date:

What is the best way to show others we love them?

Age: Date:

_____
_____
_____
_____

Age: Date:

_____
_____
_____
_____

Age: Date:

_____
_____
_____
_____

Age: Date:

_____
_____
_____
_____

What are you most thankful for and why?

Age: Date:

Age: Date:

Age: Date:

Age: Date:

How can we make the world a better place?

Age: Date:

_____
_____
_____
_____

Age: Date:

_____
_____
_____
_____

Age: Date:

_____
_____
_____
_____

Age: Date:

_____
_____
_____
_____

Kids Say and Do the Darndest Things...

Longer stories and more crazy childhood moments are recorded on the following pages.

Kids Say and Do the Darndest Things...

Kids Say and Do the Darndest Things…

Kids Say and Do the Darndest Things…

Kids Say and Do the Darndest Things…

Kids Say and Do the Darndest Things…

Kids Say and Do the Darndest Things…

Kids Say and Do the Darndest Things…

Kids Say and Do the Darndest Things…

Kids Say and Do the Darndest Things...

Kids Say and Do the Darndest Things…

Kids Say and Do the Darndest Things…

Kids Say and Do the Darndest Things…

Kids Say and Do the Darndest Things…

Kids Say and Do the Darndest Things…

Kids Say and Do the Darndest Things...

Kids Say and Do the Darndest Things…

Kids Say and Do the Darndest Things…

www.ingramcontent.com/pod-product-compliance
Lightning Source LLC
Chambersburg PA
CBHW071249070526
44583CB00017B/2388